Calculated Conflict: Part One
Generations, leadership theories and principles

Ricardo D. Wrice, Doctoral Candidate

ISBN:1979991901
ISBN-13:9781979991902

DEDICATION

It has been a long, winding journey both educational and experience wise. It amazes me that the culmination of these two has led me to this point. Calculated Conflict is a new theory that I plan to introduce to the world and this book is just part one. There are many people who have aided me in arriving here but only a few of them are key players. I would be remised if I didn't thank my amazing parents Pandrea and Richard Wrice. My grandmother, Earlee Rice and my spiritual advisor Dr. Joan Youmans. I have learned that a strong village can make all the difference. I hope this theory will help revolutionize the leadership arena and bring about a much needed shift in thinking.

CONTENTS

1 CALCULATED CONFLICT

The thought of conflict, can be a very scary one. Over the course of time, conflict has been the poster boy for strife, despair and overall discord. People have given it a bad connotation and it's almost spoken as a curse word. However, without conflict some of the greatest movements in history wouldn't exist. Nor would the biggest shifts in paradigms ever take place. Despite its connotation, conflict has a part to play in the grand design of this world.

The theory of Calculated Conflict isn't an overly complicated one. It is the belief that conflict can be anticipated or sometimes stoked to produce necessary outcomes. When done properly, conflict creates new paradigms, uncovers hidden issues and inspires innovation. Calculated Conflict takes a look at certain variables in an attempt to gain a greater insight into what's needed or warranted to spur the above outcomes.

Conflict-------Generations----------Leadership Theories & Offsets

I'm sure by now you're wondering where do I begin to start this process. First, you have to be able to decipher personal and organizational conflict. Although they differ, each one has its own set of outcomes. Next, you have to understand the players in a conflict scenario. Unlike many theories, Calculated Conflict utilizes generational research to classify players. Generational research analyzes the different age groups (Baby Boomers, Generation Y, Generation X and Millennials) and identifies their attributes. It compiles their history, work place performance, and behaviors. It gives leaders and managers the proper foresight by which to create productive atmospheres and cultures.

A look at preferred leadership styles will follow the compilation of generational research. The research will generate a specific leadership style that resonates with each generation. Lastly, you will want to become better acquainted with the different manners that offset conflict. Although it's needed, conflict can be avoided by excercising a few underutilized concepts. Calculated Conflict can help better equip you when conflict shows up at your door.

For decades, organizations have sought out world renown theorist to help solve the problem of decaying organizational standards. The consensus is almost unanimous that organizational success has to be based on a collaborative effort. Leaders as well as followers have to know that they are both valued members of the organization and that they play an intricate part in its overall success. Reciprocally, organizations have an obligation to their shareholders, the general public and their communities to ensure their continued success.

Often times, these two objectives seem mutually exclusive and almost impossible. Organizations, much like living organisms, have to continue to grow and evolve in an attempt to meet its communities growing needs and desires. Organizations have many moving parts but my plan is to examine one of its most under analyzed components, conflict.

2 THE CONFLICT CYCLE

The dictionary defines conflict as "incompatibility or interference, as of one idea, desire, event, or activity with another." Shockley-Zalaback defines conflict as a process that occurs when individuals, small groups, or organizations perceive or experience frustration in attaining goals and addressing concerns. The resolution of conflict can be the main determining factor to uncharted productivity or all-out war.

Personal Versus Organizational Conflict

The concept of this book is to help individuals learn how to better anticipate, calculate and survive conflict. Most people reading this book are probably reading it to gain a better understanding of organizational conflict. However, a parallel must be ran between personal conflict and organizational conflict.

Personal conflict refers to a breakdown or failure in communication between two or more individuals. Organizational conflict refers to a breakdown or failure of communication between an organization and its individuals. The term "organization" in this particular context, refers to the management / leadership of an organization. Unlike organizational conflict, personal conflict is a singular operating being. As a result, organizations operate under a tier leadership system revolving around a chain of command. They empower managers and supervisors to handle the operations aspect of their organizations. Often times, these empowered leaders are the only individuals in direct contact with members and supporters. They create and utilize the pipeline of communication which sets the pace for the organization.

Frustration

In both types of conflict, a breakdown or failure to communicate will lead to a sense of frustration. Frustration brings awareness that either there is a lack of communication or a failure to communicate. It is broken down into two categories: Emotional and intellectual. Emotional frustration means there is a "desire" to act but intellectual means there's a "need" to act. Personal frustration tends to be more emotionally based than organizational frustration which is more intellectually based. Operating as a singular organism, personal frustration is more prone to be led by individual emotions. For example, you will hear phrases such as "I felt" or "I thought" after experiencing personal conflict. The participants are less likely to "count up the cost" or weigh out the consequences before acting. Reciprocally, organizational frustration operates in the adverse.

Organizations operate more as a collective consisting of more thoughts, ideas and input. Their frustration, is going to be more intellectually based or members will think more collectively about their conflict outcomes. For example, you will hear phrases such as "we thought" or "we felt" after experiencing organizational conflict. They are more likely to consider variables such as: family, friends, coworkers, consequences. Emotional and intellectual frustrations are not exclusive to just one group. They can both be displayed in the opposing group and often times will be. It is important to remember that all conflict is still based off individual thoughts and actions.

The Channeling

In this outlook of conflict, frustration will lead to some form of action. Typically, either immediate action (emotional) or premeditated (intellectual) action. The channeling stage comes after the frustration stage has taken place. Personal and organizational conflict both will enter the channeling stage or action stage. During this phase, the frustration (brought about by the awareness), begins to seek outlets by which to relieve itself of the frustration. In personal conflict, individuals want immediate relief or specific questions answered. In organizational conflict, the collective desires answers or systems established to bring resolution. The channeling stage typically seeks three main outlets: Altercations, innovation, or establishment.

The altercation outlet is the least desired and the most extreme. It can be the most dangerous and least productive. In personal conflict, it can lead to fights or violent outbreaks. In organizational conflict it can lead to violence or fights.

The innovation outlet is one of the better outcomes. It is the outlet that inspires new ideas, and avenues. In personal conflict it allows individuals to see things differently. They begin to explore avenues that they wouldn't have previously considered. In organizational conflict it can usher in a new era of creativity and concepts. It helps organizations move into new areas and it allows members to reach their full potential.

The establishment outlet is definitely important for organizational conflict. The establishment outlet places boundaries and paradigms in place. In personal conflict it helps individuals create boundaries and establish standards. In organizational conflict, it creates new policies and procedures, new paradigms of thought, and it establishes protocol.

3 DECODING ORGANIZATIONAL CONFLICT

Many organizations, have been ravished by internal wars or completely decimated by its effect. In early times, conflict resolution was a major deal. Organizational issues were handled on a case-by-case basis and problems were addressed openly. In today's society, conflict has almost become a "nasty" word often times inadvertently addressed or prolonged until it turns into civil war. Organizational conflict has become cliché and organizations have become less inclined to divert resources or manpower to its diffusion. In turn, organizations will let it fester until simple mediation or negotiations cannot deflect the impeding war.

Organizational Conflict

Organizational conflict is unavoidable. The workplace is now a temporary home to many different generations, ethnicities, and genders. As a result, seldom will everyone agree to the decisions or direction by which the organization will take. The question becomes does everyone understand the organizational mission and can they find their role in the mission execution. Leadership (be it operational or executive) will rarely have the full support of their subordinates but they should strive for the mass majority. Organizational leaders, being a direct linkage to owners and shareholders, have a primary obligation to ensure the interest of those in power. Often times, they are taught that this obligation trumps their allegiance to their subordinates. As a result, the needs and desires of the status quo go unfulfilled or unheard. Left unchecked, this neglect can lead to the instigation of civil war within an organization.

Organizational Civil War

A organizational civil war refers to an internal war between factions within an organization trying to create, or derail management for the entire organization or some territorial part of it. Despite the general belief, organizational civil war doesn't start overnight. The formation of factions isn't an overnight process either. As an individual who has worked in many different sectors, I can attest that often times faction creation is a snowball effect. It begins with one individual voicing a general opinion or a slight "oversight" and from there it becomes "discussion". If the issue isn't addressed, the "finger pointer" revisits the issue and places it back on the table.

Meanwhile, the other employees secretly await a response from management. The absence of a reaction or response has now presented the image of not caring. In turn, employees begin to re-evaluate the way they perceive the company and its management. Meanwhile, at the water cooler word has traveled about the "lack of action" and it sparks re-evaluation in a neighboring department. A lack of action, is the fastest way to ignite an inferno of leadership re-evaluation. In this scenario, action should have been taken to extinguish the flames of discontent. If not, this "simple" issue turns into a organizational divider between management and employees.

4 CONFLICT SOURCES

The above scenario is just one instance of how organizational conflict can begin. The belief that "negativity" is some spirit that can be magically exiled is an illusion and not a good one. In some regard, conflict is liking to the development of a tree. The use of seeds, the ground, and tilling are all valid connotations. The employees are the seeds, your company culture is the ground and your profits, productivity and morale are the harvest. Often times, managers are unaware of the root factors causing conflict and that places them at a disadvantage in the workplace. Organizational Conflict can be sparked by many different things but there are a few significant sparks.

Common Conflict Sources

Leading the charge on conflict sources is organizational change. Instinctively, humans are genetically resistant to any level of change. Depending on their background, accepting change becomes a process. Company change may uncover many hidden variables such as: resource scarcity, burnout, strained relationships, job dissatisfaction, or decayed company loyalty. Organizational change is inevitable and organizational members must be considered during the process.

Organizational turnover or downsizing

For the last couple of years we have seen the economy crash and recover. Companies going under, almost became the norm and it left millions with nowhere to go. This level of change, can leave employees skeptical about company politics. Many develop a distrust for management and find it hard to re develop company loyalty.

Leadership / management changes

The changing of leadership can be hard for employees to grapple with. Especially older employees who have developed bonds and built trust with old management. A change in management can be the most fragile change possible and it can destroy an organization. Employee trust is vital to not only the success of an organization but to the management as well. In order to produce desired results, management has to garner the respect and trust of their subordinates.

Merging and Company Dissolution

Growth and expansion are the "bread and butter" of any organization. As a result, mergers and acquisitions have become increasingly popular. This particular process, is one of the harder transitions for all parties involved. By nature, a merger almost requires the creation of a completely new organization. However, this new creation becomes bits and pieces of the old ones. The "creation" process is the quickest to isolate people or leave too many questions. Unanswered questions, can result in employees being led by their own thoughts which can rapidly change their perception.

These three examples, are not the only ways to define organizational change but they can be the hardest to navigate. It takes a collaborative effort on behalf of both management and employees to keep the lines of communication open.

5 THE GENERATIONAL PLAYERS

In a historical turn, America has four generations of people integrated into the workforce. Although it offers its share of benefits, organizations are now challenged with accommodating these different generations. A generation is a group that shares an identity based on birth years and significant life events. These life events can range from wars, to natural disasters, significant technological developments and innovation.

The notion is that the culmination of both their years and life events makes each generation's outlook unique. A lack of generational understanding, can prove detrimental along the lines of communication and workplace relationships. Organizational leaders are tasked with creating environments that attract and cultivate each generation.

Baby-Boomers

The baby-boomer generation consists of children born between 1946 and 1964. The baby boomer birth rate soared between World War II and the Great Depression. As a result, they are the largest generation in American history. Baby boomers are seen as both resourceful and opportunistic. The effects of their life events created a need for individuality and a desire to challenge authority. This need for individuality, eventually led to civil unrest sparking movements such as the Civil Rights riots.

Boomers in the Workforce

The boomers grew up in a more traditional parental setting. The father was considered the sole household provider and the mother was the housewife. This household dynamic, led boomers to value their jobs. In the workforce boomers are considered loyal and competitive. They make career sacrifices and value their concept of hard work (long hours, and job dedication). Baby boomers are team oriented and value having a strong work ethic. Boomers are content maintaining the company policies versus challenging the way procedures are executed. Despite the contention, boomers are continual learners and have a "thirst" for knowledge.

Generation X

The Generation X individuals were born between 1965 and 1981. They are the generation that was birth after the baby boomers and into a challenging new economy. This generation was ushered in on the heels of the Cold War, the AIDS epidemic and organizational scandals. Parented by baby boomers, this generation was raised by mass media and technology. Generation X individuals seek to retain balance in both their professional and personal lives. The exposure to organizational scandal has forged low company loyalty and a particular distrust for them.

Generation X in the Workplace

Generation X's outlook on the workforce is skewed with the memories of working parents. They were the first generation to witness both parents working. In the absence of parental units, Generation X children acquired an independence and adaptability mindset. They adopted a "work hard, play hard" ideology which encouraged a balance in the two arenas. Witnessing their parents lose their jobs in a bad economy, this generation discarded company loyalty.

Generation X is motivated to achieve and have no issue taking risk. They maintain a loyalty to coworkers and bosses than to the actual organization. In turn, these individuals maneuver through employment seeking the next best opportunity. A good quality of life is a primary focus for this generation and they desire to both lead and follow. Unlike boomers, Generation X prefers to work alone and avoid team work.

Generation Y

Generation Y are individuals born between 1977 and 1997. The Generation Y group is heavily into technology. Their worldly outlook has been shaped by the September 11th terrorist attacks, the Persian Gulf war, natural disasters and the introduction of the internet. This generation, was born to older parents and maintains a sense of civic duty. Having been birth after boomers and Generation X, this generation has a "blended" view. Generation Y witnessed overworked and underappreciated grandparents. As a result, they adopted a similar mindset to the previous generation

X. They desire flexible working schedules and the accommodations for their technology.

Generation Y in the Workplace

Generation Y seeks tolerance in the workplace and they utilize a positive can do- ideology. They place high levels of trust in authority and welcome the team work experience. Their love for technology has created a "group" mentality and they prefer group task. They benefit the most from mentorship and relationships. They seek to establish connections with not only each other but their leaders as well.

Unlike Generation X, Generation Y is not an independent generation. They require more structure, attention and afore knowledge. They can be perceived as high maintenance employees requiring immediate feedback and attention. GenerationY individuals are great multi-taskers and are motivated by the passion to be more personally marketable. They seek to partake in meaningful work and contribute to the greater good. Monetary compensation ranks lower on their hierarchy compared to civic duty.

The Millennial

The last generation is the millennials or individuals born between 1982 and 2000. Outside of the baby boomers, this generation is the fastest growing group. They value education, are highly confident, able to multi-task well and are self sustaining. The millennials had the advantage of knowledge from the previous three generations and they were accommodated. The last two generations (X and Y) maintained balance to ensure this generation would understand family values. Similar to Generation Y, millennial are tech savvy and are masters of social networking. They encourage group interactions and have a desire to fulfill civic duty.

Millennials in the Workplace

In the workforce, millennials utilize more technology and prefer group dynamics. They desire to utilize technology to unravel complicated and illusive questions. They are creative and socially minded. This particular generation has become the victims of a world created to appease them. Organizational leaders find that millennials struggle in environments devoid of structure, or any level of ambiguity. They are accustomed to set perimeters, deadlines and examples.

Millennials expectations in the workplace are based on open communication. Their main objective is to maintain a steady flow of information. In order to achieve this flow, millennials seek to build close relationships with their supervisors. Unlike baby boomers, need-to-know information flows are not acceptable. They desire to be constantly kept in the know down to the smallest detail. To millennials, group-based work is perceived as more fun and elevates risk. Millennials preference for media outlets has presented new challenges for organizations. The engagement of millennials is centered on the allowance of creativity and utilization of their ideas.

6 LEADERSHIP STYLE AND WORK TEAMS PERFORMANCE

Organizational leaders have a new challenge presented to them in this seemingly diversified workplace. Diversity is no longer limited to just ethnicities and cultures. Leaders now have to learn how to develop and support a productive multigenerational team. To accomplish this task, leaders must understand the various needs of each generation and adhere to them. The avoidance of conflict and miscommunication amongst the generations is considered top priority.

Baby Boomers

Being the oldest generation, boomers can also be the least fluid. Their level of productivity is founded on organizational commitment and stability. This generation, is more adapt to more of a transactional style of leadership. Transactional leadership is a process exchange between an organization and its employees. Transactional leader's main desire is to keep the organization running properly at all cost. They are less concerned with change and place stability as a top priority. Boomers main goal is to service the organization in exchange for employment stability.

In a team environment, boomers are better served in a mentoring capacity. Their contentment with company sacrifice, is an attribute that would keep a group focused on the "transaction" at hand. Reciprocally, their lack of balance could cause a divide when it comes to task execution. Boomers tend to place the company needs above their own whereas the other three generations maintain balance. Baby boomers are not conflict oriented. Group dynamics are a breeding ground for conflict and boomers are indirect confronters. They prefer to solely focus on the transaction at hand and they are less concerned with the details to achieve the objective.

Generation X

In contrast with the baby boomers, Generation X is almost the complete opposite. Generation X individuals are self-sustainers. They promote independence and are self-motivators. Their self-motivation, leads them to be loyal to a profession versus a particular organization. They seek opportunities to transform themselves and sharpen their skill sets. For this cause, they respond better to transformational leadership styles. Transformational leadership is the changing or "transforming" of people's lives or mindsets. Transformational leaders assess the motives, needs and goals of their followers.

In a team environment, generation x individuals make good group leaders. They are more relationship oriented and prefer to build relationships with their followers. Their passion for a profession takes precedence over any particular organizations needs. As a result they can help create experts within organizations and the field. Generation X individuals welcome diversity and like to challenge their coworkers. Although they prefer working alone, they can both lead and follow effectively.

Generation Y

Generation Y is a more technology savvy generation. They exemplify technical abilities, understand the power of social media and they stay connected. They grew up during a time of globalization, social media and this has helped shape their outlook. Generation Y is seeking external satisfaction and relevant work. They desire attention and constant feedback on their promotional status. Generation Y is less concerned with job satisfaction and more concerned with lifestyle. This generation responds better to both transformational and situational leadership. Situational Leadership implies that no one particular approach can fit every situation or dilemma.

In the workplace, Generation Y has grown accustomed to team work which may include globalized teams with virtual communication. This generation is the first generation to utilize research, practice methods and outcome data. They have a higher level of understanding of team diversity and it helps enhance their marketability. In a team they can help facilitate the information flow and research efforts. Their preference for newer forms of communication (emails, texting, skyping), makes team communication easier and more efficient.

Millennials

The millennials grew up in a fast paced, ever changing world. Unlike Generation Y, millennials didn't mature into technology. They have come to expect it and it is incorporated into their everyday life. Wisniewski (2010) contends that this generation cannot be engaged by typical paper and pencil approaches to learning. They understand technology and desire to utilize it to better their lives. The Situational style of leadership is best suited to engage this generation. This style of leadership, leads based on the specific needs and variables of a particular situation. Millennials are less concerned with organizational objectives and more concerned with cultivating environments.

In the workplace, millennials (much like Generation Y) are more concerned with a lifestyle than job satifaction. They welcome group work and are sensitive to the needs of other ethnicities. Millennials are digital natives that excel areas such as multi-tasking, visual stimulation and information filtering. They have almost mastered video chatting, which enables them to participate in a virtual groups. Due to the smartphone, they can be reached at a moments notice. Reciprocally, unlike baby boomers millennials aren't interested in "climbing the corporate ladder". They are seeking organizations that promote quickly and provide minimal training.

7 LEADERSHIP THEORIES

As you can see, there is a lot of information and insight when it comes to the different generations. Generational research is a very powerful tool to help navigate the very rigorous tide of human capital. There is no way to completely understand the thought process of any one individual but generational research helps bring insight. The major advantage of this type of research is its universal insight. Generational research crosses all ethnicities, orientation, and genders. It is especially good for collective leading because it has already grouped individuals by their age.

This particular chapter continues the process of leading these different generations. Continuing from the last chapter, I want to give a foundational understanding to the leadership styles mentioned for each group. My objective is to not only simplify each style but to also present other notes as well. Understanding these leadership styles, will make a leader/managers job less grueling

Maslow's Hierachy of Needs

It is important to build a good foundation when discussing the needs of followers and how to meet those needs. For this cause, I want to open this chapter discussing Maslow's Hierarchy of Needs. Created in 1943, Abraham Maslow introduced the Hierarchy of Needs theory. It was his belief that individual's needs should be met at their most basic level and compounded until their highest level is reached. Maslow utilized the pyramid shape to execute his point, placing the most basic needs at the bottom. He categorized the pyramid into to three groups: Basic needs, Psychological needs and Self-fulfillment needs.

Basic Needs

Basics needs are classified as air, water, food and shelter. Although considered basic, these particular needs are necessary to begin the "securing" process. In keeping with the diagram, managers and leaders have to secure each category before moving on to the next. It is also important to remember that each of these "levels" may look different to each generation. For instance, let's use rest (which is at the bottom). Baby boomers are more accustomed to working long hours and maintaining company loyalty. Millennials are the opposite and they operate as such.

Given this scenerio, a leader would have to develop two different schedules. For Baby boomers, they may schedule them 40+ hours a week. For their millennial staff, they may schedule them less but place them on call. As a result, you are accounting for the level of rest each generation may desire based on the afore knowledge you now possess. It is important to remember that this information is designed to be intermingled and correlated to create better leaders. Although the needs may be the same, the meeting of those needs will have to be taylored to your particular group of followers.

Psychological Needs

Decades ago, leaders only had the task of making sure people's basic needs were met. They made sure they had proper pay, pensions, job satisfaction and good hours. In today's society, we've shifted to focusing more on the work environment. This shift can be accredited to the changing of house hold dynamics, and people's job desires evolving. I would venture to say that tending to your followers psychological needs has become a number one priority.

In keeping with this belief, individuals want to feel like they "belong" to something bigger. In today's environments / workplaces this has become especially important when it comes to millennials. Unlike the previous generations (Baby Boomers in particular), millennials want to feel valued in an organization. The emergence of social media now creates a longing to be included and connected at all times. Organizations that fail to create an all-inclusive company culture will have major problems with retention.

Included in this particular category is prestige & accomplishments. Organizational members still find value in being rewarded and recognized for their hard work. Later in the book I will cover company culture and company loyalty. Organizations that fail to honor and reward members are destined to not keep them around very long. At its core, culture and loyalty are built off the appreciation of the members. It becomes imperative that organizations create environments and cultures that foster appreciation.

Self-Fulfillment

At the top of the pyramid is the self-fulfillment category. It is at the top because it signifies that one has reached their full potential or realized their purpose. Although this theory is in the shape of a pyramid, the needs can be interchangeable depending on the individual. The fulfillment or self-actualization stage will typically be individually based. Only the individual can decide how they see their "best self" and adjust accordingly. Organizations can offer programs and services to help members learn and develop to lead them to this final stage. This stage is also an ever evolving stage and not the final stage of development. Maslow's needs table allows leaders to grasp a clearer picture of where to start with meeting member's needs. Leaders must first understand the most basic needs of their members if they are ever to be successful.

Leadership Styles

So far we have talked about generations, member's needs and the conflict process. All of these variables will lead you to discovering your leadership style. In this chapter, I want to look at the four different styles of leadership which are: Servant Leadership, Transformational Leadership, Transactional Leadership and Situational Leadership. The chapter on the generations discussed the preference for each generation and these were their preferences.

Servant Leadership

I am going to cover Servant leadership first because I don't teach it as an independent leadership style. It is one of the few styles that I don't feel should be taught alone because it is more of a foundational principle. Robert Greenleaf created this concept in 1970 and it still holds some truth to this day. Servant leadership states that the leader is to be a servant first before they can be an effective leader. He felt that serving should come naturally to a leader and that everything comes second. He also felt that the needs of the people should be of the highest priority and people's growth is the goal. Traditionally, leadership is a "from the top down" type of arrangement but Servant leadership is the opposite. A servant leader shares power and places the needs of others above all else.

People First, Leading Second

One of the major problems I am seeing with this theory, is the perception that people come first and leading is second. As a result, these types of leaders are only developing one particular skill set and neglecting to nurture the other areas. Servant Leaders are now doing their subordinates a great disservice by failing to perfect their crafts. Particularly, in the third sector where this theory is the cornerstone for training / equipping the next generation of leaders. The third sector is where you will find more of your low income projects, churches and other nonprofit organizations.

The notion of "people first, lead second" seems to be some unwritten rule and it is producing ineffective leaders in the "business" aspects of these organizations. I absolutely believe that people are vital to any organization but I also believe that the absence of a villain (or tough decision maker) will be detrimental. Leaders have to understand that leading will not always make them popular nor will their organization run itself. Even in churches, the belief that a celestial being is going to magically rectify their poor operating decisions is unrealistic.

Not An Independent Theory

Observing what has transpired in this new age leadership, I don't believe that the Servant Leadership Theory should be taught independently. In my opinion, it should be taught in conjunction with another theory preferably the Transactional Leadership Theory. Transactional Leadership focuses more on supervision, organization and performance. In essence, creating a balance between it and the Servant Leadership Theory. Transactional Leadership would call for leaders to focus equally on the supervising and leading aspect of leadership. Reciprocally, Servant Leadership would allow leaders to stay connected to their subordinates. Thus, allowing new leaders to create a healthy and productive hybrid of the two theories.

Transactional Leadership

In 1947, Max Weber created the style known as Transactional leadership. It is a style built on managers exchanging needs with employees. It conforms to an existing organizational structure and measures success according to rewards and penalties. Transactional leaders have formal authority and positions of responsibility in an organization. In other words, they lead by metrics and results.

In keeping with our generational research, Baby Boomers respond well to this type of leadership. Primarily because it is very "black and white" versus the "gray" that other generations may prefer. Transactional leadership holds true to its origin word which is "transaction" and it operates as such. They prefer that everyone understand their job and be awarded or penalized accordingly.

Little Wiggle Room

In my synopsis of Servant leadership, I conceded that it should be taught in conjunction with this style. Transactional leadership brings a certain level of authority to the Servant leader module and that is the missing link.

Reciprocally, Transactional leadership is a style that is more befitting for certain types of organizations. For example, larger organizations, military organizations or organizations that operate off quotas and rubrics. It is typically not a good fit for nonprofits, or smaller organizations where responsibilities can be more fluid.

At its core, Transactional leadership focuses more on the "telling" versus the "selling" style. It tends to play more to the self-interest of an individual and less about to the collective. In essence, leaving little wiggle room to develop skill sets and abilities.

Transformational Leadership

Transformational Leadership was created by James MacGregor Burns in 1978. It is the process by which leaders and followers help each other to advance to a higher level of morale and motivation. Transformational leaders strive to change through example and they look to challenge goals. They seek to inspire and motivate members to strive to be the best version of themselves. Unlike transactional leadership, transformational leadership is better suited for many organizations especially nonprofits. These types of leaders create positive change in their followers and develop them into leaders. Unlike the previous two styles, Transformational leadership has very few drawbacks.

Situational Leadership

In 1985, Blanchard and Hersey developed the Situational Leadership style. The name pretty much says it all. This is the most flexible style of leadership created. It is a troubleshooting style which adapts to the existing work environment and the needs of the organization. Situational leaders don't dwell on their particular skillset but they modify their management style to better suit their organization. In my personal opinion, this style of leadership requires the most insight. Situational leaders have to be able to access a situation and decide the best management style to fit the need.

8 CONFLICT OFFSETS

Calculating conflict can be a very strategic process. Throughout the book, I spoke about the different variables involved in the formula. However, there are many old school remedies for avoiding this level of conflict. I would like to discuss a few.

Company Loyalty

When I was a child, my father worked for a local plant in our small town. The town, was a country town with about one stop light and no Walmart. At the time, the company would have a "bring your family to work" day. It was an all-day event in which the company would hire local vendors to set up fun carnival type booths, local djs to provide the music and we got to see what our parents did all day. Looking back, im sure that the event was beyond costly but it was a worthy investment. This company not only fulfilled its social responsibility but it also groomed the next generation of workers. The community embraced the company and it became a lifeline to many of the residents in the town.

In the end, the company and the community created a bond that was unbreakable for years. From just this one event, the company was able to ensure its continued success in the neighborhood and it secured an unspoken allegiance to its longevity.

Company loyalty is a necessity for any company planning to grow and thrive. The notion of loyalty, eludes to a sense of mutual respect and a sort of bond. It implies a willingness from two parties to always keep the best interest of each other and keep the lines of communication open. Company loyalty insists that companies always keep the best interest of their employees and make decisions accordingly. In return, employees vow to stay true to the mission and objectives created by the organization.

The above example, is just one scenario of how companies can build and maintain company / brand loyalty. My father's company only had this event one time a year but it became a staple in the community. Families, companies and individuals began to look forward to the event and they made it a bigger affair every year. The connection between human capital and social responsibility is a very delicate one.

The communities in which businesses operate should be their primary focus. These communities, provide not only resources (building, utilities, etc.) but also clientele and potential employees. Particularity communities where skills are limited and education isn't a priority. Companies that take the time to build relationships within their operating communities find operating a little less taxing.

Company Culture

Ions ago, organizations fought hard to retain and train the best talent available. Talented individuals came out of college knowing what organizations they wanted to work for and they set their sights on getting in. Organizations realized that people were the most important element and they adjusted accordingly. Fast forward almost a century later and the tide has definitely changed. The bottom line has changed and so has the endgame for many organizations. Terms like pensions, retirement and even

Christmas parties have become a thing of the past. Reciprocally, the desires of employees has changed dramatically and now money truly rules the game.

Human Capital

First things first, what is human capital? It is the skills, knowledge, and experience possessed by an individual or population, viewed in terms of their value or cost to an organization or country. In a nutshell, it's the human side to any organization. Despite today's take on it, human capital is an investment. Organizations place their money, and time into creating an individual that will become a human asset to their business. Let's look at it more closely:

Schedule the interview----Interview---2nd interview----paid training----uniform----probationary period (all paid)

The above diagram is just a snapshot of the money that goes into hiring one individual for your organization. Keep in mind, that someone is being paid to perform all those duties up until the person is hired. Imagine the amount money that goes into this process when a company has a low retention rate. Retention refers to the ability of an organization to "retain" or keep their employees for long periods of time. Low retention means that an organization is constantly hiring or looking for new employees on a consistent basis. In the grand scheme of things, companies are loosing millions on the high turn over rates of their employees. For smaller companies, this can be the difference between a profits quarter or a quarter full of loses.

The Offset

Despite the myth, retention is not solely the job of your Human Resources department. Honestly, it falls on the executive and operations managers to create a company culture that fosters appreciation and respect for the employees. Company culture encompasses values and behaviors that contribute to the unique social and psychological environment of an organization. In other words, it is the atmosphere of a workplace that creates the standard by which employees will operate.

Devoid of a culture, employees will create their own standard and that will be created by the status quo. Allowing the status quo to create that culture, places the future of the organization in the hands of individuals who all think alike. These individuals, may or may not have the best interest of the organization and they can create a revolving door for employees.

It would behoove companies to take the time to properly groom potential talent to move into management. Properly groomed managers, can help create and maintain a company culture that can offset losses in Human Capital.

The feedback Scenario

As human beings, we all have a desire to belong to something greater and to feel valued in that "something". Abraham Maslow had the right idea when he placed belonging / love in the middle of his hierarchy of needs. There is a subtle power in making people feel like they are a part of something great and creating a safe space for their development. As leaders, it is important to understand that you cannot please everyone but you do still have that obligation. The obligation is to set the standard and create the culture. It should be a culture where thoughts, ideas and concerns are considered. More importantly, these elements should be heavily considered and executed on some level.

The Feedback Process

The biggest gripe I have ever heard in an organization is "they don't listen to us" or "they don't care about us". These two phrases are typically the catalyst for civil war or the beginning of the end. In the best offset, organizations will then solicit feedback. The solicitation of feedback can be your best ally depending on your intention.

Often times, organizations solicit feedback as a silencer or just to "shut up the masses". They have no intent on actually executing any of the doable suggestions because they already have their own set agenda. In this case, feedback is a just a formality and it won't lead to any real change. There is a certain level of empowerment that comes with being asked for your feedback and the acknowledgment of that feedback.

The "silencer" scenario is the most dangerous and can literally lead to the downfall of your organization. I can assure you there is nothing more dangerous than the creation of a deprived faction.

The key in a feedback situation is to: Actually listen (not just hear), plan to execute and acknowledge. First, organizational leadership has to actually listen and engage in a feedback scenario and that may lead to some harsh realities. Remember your followers see and experience things on a different level. As a result, leadership has to be receptive and open to possible criticism as well as praise.

Next, plan to actually execute the "good" or "possible" suggestions. Often times, your follows don't care which suggestion you take. They just want to see some level of change based off their ideas and suggestions.

Lastly, acknowledge where the feedback came from and how it helped initiate some type of change. Organizations will be amazed at how fast the feedback process can change the morale and rejuvenate your follows. It is one of the fastest and least expensive ways to redirect a failing organization.

9 SUMMARY

I created Calculated Conflict to help shine a light into the ever changing world of leadership. The world is ever changing and technology is constantly elevating our evolution. It is my desire to restore and create new avenues by which to lead. Before I end this first book, there are a few nuggets I want to leave you with.

First, conflict is necessary. I hope that after reading through this book you now have a greater respect for the term. Healthy conflict is the remedy for some of the world's most underachieving companies.

Secondly, generational research can be your best friend if you let it. The information that you learned from Chapter 5, should empower you to change your approach. I advise looking into this research further. My second book will also add Generation Z which is the next generation.

Lastly, although conflict isn't terrible it can sometimes be avoided by old school concepts. The last chapter may have sounded cliché but many companies have forgotten those practices. A return to some of those offsets can make the difference between a thriving company and a destroyed one.

In conclusion, I hope that you have not only learned something but enjoyed the journey. It is my desire to train and equip the next generation of leaders. This book is just the beginning of my many ideals on leadership. I look forward to sharing more of my theories in the future.

www.ingramcontent.com/pod-product-compliance
Lightning Source LLC
Chambersburg PA
CBHW030037230526
45472CB00002B/554